A Century of Motorcycling in Cornwall

Compiled by Roger Fogg
Published by: Blue Hills Publishing
Reprinted 2005

The Cornish Flag is raised and saluted at
the 1992 ISDE in Holland by Tony Jury,
whilst Olly Lamper looks on.

ACKNOWLEDGEMENTS.

This book is a celebration of the motorcycle and its variants - the scooter, the sidecar and the three wheeled car in the County of Cornwall. It has been a labour of love, sometimes lust. I have spent many hours chasing photographs, wrestling with word processors and e-mails, researching and talking. I have to say that the knowledge and enthusiasm that exists within the world of motorcycles is exceptional. So many people have given of their time as well as their treasured photographs. It would be invidious of me to single out too many individuals, but special mention must be made of Tom and Mark Seward, Sally Madgwick, Peter Henshaw and Peter Old. Where possible I have tried to acknowledge the source of the images. I have acquired some photographs from jumble sales, car boots, auctions and autojumbles, and it's just not easy to attribute a source to some of these. If I have inadvertently infringed copyright in this publication I apologise and will try to redress that issue if it comes up. I have not been able to use some really good pictures that appeared in contemporary magazines because of the cost of the copyright; fair enough, but a pity. Inevitably I will have made mistakes with the captions, and someone will no doubt point out the errors, but I have tried to double check the accuracy of the statements with people who know about these things. Louise Hillier has been invaluable to the creation of this book, not only through her skills as a graphic designer but for her enthusiasm, advice and contacts. The panel contains a list of people (in no special order) who have provided images, stories and above all time to help produce this short history of my favourite form of transport in the best County of all. I cannot thank them enough. If there are any I have missed out please accept my apologies.

Ian Thompson, Sam Edyvean, Tom Seward, Mark Seward, Charlie Williams, Eric Tregonning, Boo Cock, Peter Sandry, Peter Old, Mervyn Pearce, Andrew Northam, Elizabeth and David Jobsen, Martin Curl, Don White, Marilyn Thompson, Colin Vincent, Morcom Moyle, Frances Brewer, Les Willis, Alan Wakeford, Harry Ross, Cornwall Centre ACU, Koben Triggs, Emlyn Evans, Sally Madgwick, Stan Weston, Louise Hillier, Roger Maddever, Kate Sicolo, Dave Hills, Tiffany Coates, Ted Barrett, Gary Prisk, Phil Farrar, Andrew Milton, Gary Gillum, Tom and Sarah Franks, Julia Jennings, The V.M.C.C., Ally Clift, Alan Benallick, Peter Henshaw, Dave Howells, John Deacon's family, Pinnacle Photography, Nick Palmer, Lloyd Watson, Matt Jessop Photography, Action Sport Photography and above all Mid Cornwall Brokers of Bodmin

Published by: Blue Hills Publishing Tel: 01726 67198

ISBN 0-9549005-0-2

Typesetting and Design: Louise Hillier Designs,

1 Trevaunance Cove, St Agnes, Cornwall, TR5 0SA,

Tel: 01872 553613, E-Mail: loo@zoom.co.uk

Can you imagine these going over Bodmin Moor?

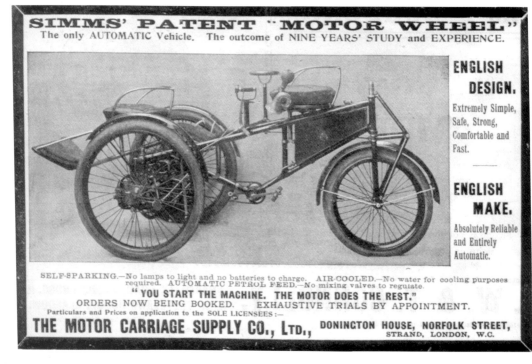

A Century of Motorcycling in Cornwall
A brief history

The Early Years

In Cornwall, at the end of the 19th century, few people travelled outside their immediate environment unless obliged to do so. Transport was at a premium and confined mainly to horse and cart, ship or railway. Towards the end of the Victorian era all this began to change with the invention of the internal combustion engine and its application as a means of individualised and mass transport. No one knows exactly when the first motorcycle was invented although the first workable machine that was produced in any volume was the Hildebrand and Wolfmuller, made in Germany in 1894. In the same year, an Englishman, Edward Butler patented a design for a motorised two wheeler. However he had been handicapped by the Road Acts of 1861 and 1865 which required self-propelled vehicles to be limited to 4mph, and preceeded on foot by a person carrying a red flag.

In France and Germany there were no such restrictions and development of the petrol-engined vehicle continued apace. New designs of cars, motorcycles, tricycles and quads appeared almost daily. However it was not until 1901 that the French engineers who made the Werner finally found the best place to put the engine. Previous locations included handlebars, behind the rear wheel and in the front hub. Werners put their engine where the pedals are on a bicycle, thereby obtaining a low centre of gravity that was essential to stop the frail machine from top-pling over or skidding, with often disastrous results.

Cornish roads were still very poor at the time, consisting in the main of rolled stone liberally sprinkled with mud, horse droppings, horseshoe nails and other agricultural detritus. Often the roads consisted of three well worn tracks with grass separating them, this being caused by a pair of cartwheels with a groove formed by iron shod hooves up the middle. In the winter these became a quagmire and in the summer dust was a huge hazard. Horse riders and their mounts objected to the new fangled forms of transport and responded with both whip and hoof.

In the early 1900s a ride on a motorcycle was a voyage of adventure. Before starting, checks had to be made. Was there enough petrol? There were no filling stations as we know them now; motor spirit had to be obtained from chemists who sold it in tins, or it had to be ordered in bulk from somewhere up the line and delivered to the nearest station by train. Was the battery charged and securely fastened to the frame? Here it was subject to much vibration, causing the casing to split and leak acid all over the place, including the rider's trousers, causing holes to inexplicably appear in the most inconvenient places.

Was there enough carbide for the lamps should a journey in the dark be necessary, and were there enough tools (carried on the riders back) to cope with the almost inevitable breakdown?

COMPETITIONS AND IMPROVEMENT

When the Red Flag Act was finally repealed and vehicles were able to travel at any speed they wished, many different makes came into being in the hope of exploiting a potential market that was clearly there for the taking. Manufacturers gained early publicity by sponsoring riders to break the record for the time taken to travel from John O Groats to Lands End non stop. This in part reflected

the great races between cities and countries that at the time were going on on the continent and which ended with the famous 1903 Paris Madrid race.

In July 1902 E H Arnott on a 2hp French Werner did the run in 65 hours 45 minutes. This in turn was gradually pared down by speedsters such as G P Mills, Arthur Bentley (the brother of W O Bentley of car fame), and Ivan Hart Davies. Speeds rose rapidly. The police became excited. Hart Davies' final official effort involved the use of other riders often dressed in white and placed at tricky road junctions or on the edges of towns showing him the way through so that he would lose no time. He rode the end to end course on a belt-driven Triumph in a time of 29 hours 12 minutes. This is the last time that this record was officially recognised because the attempts to break it were becoming a public menace. This interlude, in which the hotel at Lands End figured so prominently in the minds of riders close to the absolute edge of exhaustion is worthy of a place in the annals of a sport which has inspired so much

courage, skill and perseverance.

Joe Lobb remembers; "When my grandfather was young, it was in the early 1900's because I'm eighty now, he got a new motorcycle. He ordered it from the factory-it was something called a Quadrant and it arrived by train in Camborne. He was very proud of his new bike and once he got the hang of it he loved to show off to his friends. He was very keen on a young lady from out Stithians way, and she liked him but was not too sure about his chosen means of locomotion. In order to lure her out with him for the day, my grandfather got a 'Whippet' trailer, - you could buy them specially to pull behind a motorbike or three-wheeler. It was nicely sprung, made of cane and had red upholstery

Anyway he persuaded this young lady, against her better judgement, to get in the trailer and go for a ride with him. All went well for a while, except that is for the noxious exhaust fumes and general rural detritus kicked up by the back wheel that tended to smother his sweetie's second best coat. Rounding a sharp bend however the strain became too much for the trailer connection and it suddenly and without warning gave way. The motorcycle, freed from its burden, took a sudden leap forward, leaving the unfortunate trailerist tipped completely backwards, waving the prettiest pair of ankles in the air, as she, her petticoats, handbag and parasol all screeched to a halt in the mud of a farm gate. It was a slow speed occurrence and there were no injuries except that of pride. The lady departed by horse and cart, never to return, After that Grandfather sold the trailer and fitted a sidecar. He then wooed another girl, who had not heard of the trailer incident, and the upshot was that he married the lady, my grandmother."

Josiah Jenkin of St Austell was an early motorcyclist. He had one of the first motorcycles in Cornwall. In time he got to be a recognized authority on the internal combustion engine and started a career dealing with the motorised bicycles of others in the area. Known as Siah, the pictures show him on a 1903 Matchless with one of the very first sidecars. (left) They were in fact only invented in that year. The later Bradbury (above) still remains in the family.

T. Seward

7

The reason for putting this photograph in this book despite the fact that it was not taken in Cornwall, is that the Hough family moved to Mevagissey and lived at Polstreath for many years. It shows a trio of Excelsior-engined machines, and illustrates how an early attempt at carrying passengers involved removing the front forks of a motorcycle and substituting two wheels with a wicker chair. This device was known as a forecar, and in that state did not last long as a means of transport, being inferior to the sidecar. This photograph was taken from a glass negative.

1903 De Dion-engined Large, Paris-Madrid racer, photographed near its St. Austell home.

1908 Rex, known as the King of the Motorcycles. This pair were photographed in Truro. It is worth noting their furry hats and gloves and the passenger's waterproof cover protecting his legs.

A 1912 BSA at the mid morning stop whilst taking part in the 2004 London to Brighton Pioneer Run. This bike is owned by a gentleman from Scotland, but is believed to be one of the hoard of machines which came from Prowses garage in Penzance.

A 1916 Radco, made in Birmingham. These little Two-Strokes were popular as a cheap but reliable means of transport. In Cornwall they were sold through agencies such as Taylors Garage of Coinagehall Street, Penzance and Williamsons Garage of Church Street, Camborne.

Ivan Hart Davies on his record breaking Lands End to John'o Groats Triumph at the door of The Lands End Hotel in 1911.

The 1906/7 NSU owned by Hawkins Motors of St Stephen. This should have NSU's own leading link forks, instead of the more practical Bramptons fitted, but is an exceptional survivor, having stayed in the same village for most of its life.

Scotts were very advanced for their time, having clutch, kick start and excellent pulling power. This is Charlie Williams's 1912 machine in storage at Redruth.

Above: An early Triumph with its wicker sidecar in place.
Left: This may be AF746 which was first registered by John Jackson of Lanner as a CH JAP TT Roadster.

Above: Old motorcycles could be improved, and the place to test them was the Goss Moor. If a three-speed gearbox was fitted as well as a Sturmey Archer three-speed hub then a fair turn of speed could be obtained despite the low revving engines. It really was true that they fired once every telegraph pole.

I had no petrol and the Nipper whistled "Home, Sweet Home."

THE FIRST WORLD WAR

By the end of 1913 there were nearly 100,000 motorcycles in use in Britain. Within a span of a few years the motorcycle had become a thoroughly reliable, go anywhere machine. Gear boxes, clutches, chain drive, kick starts, electric lighting had all become available. A motorcycle had become an affordable means of transport, and with sidecar attached was one by which the whole family could use to go shopping, visit friends and relatives or simply to go away on holiday. Cornwall was beginning to see the start of the motorised tourist market.

Many local garages sprang up to meet demand. They catered not just for a particular make or type of vehicle, but were agents for a wide variety of cars, motorcycles and a wonderful assortment of oddities that were being experimented with at the time.

As the First World War approached it became obvious that the motorcycle would play an important role. Triumph and Douglas were amongst the most popular marques chosen for dispatch riding duties around the Western Front, other manufacturers such as P and M, Clyno, Enfield and Scott all made combinations that were used for fire fighting, stretcher bearing and as machine gun platforms.

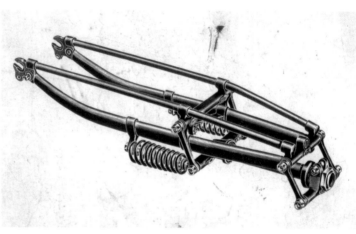

AF 1368 a $2^{3}/4$ hp Douglas registered on 8th March 1915 by Lieut. T Ginman, 7th Royal Fusiliers, Porthleven, Cornwall for Military Purposes.

A Model H Triumph, ex-military, converted for civilian use and used to convey this gentleman from Probus College to his golf club.

THE VINTAGE YEARS, 1918-1930

The war years had proved a testing time for all the countries involved, and not least for the machines with which the war had been fought.

The motorcycle emerged tougher, more practical and more reliable than ever before. The end of the fighting signalled what was for many the golden age of motorcycling in this country, and the start of a new and prosperous era for the industry.

Immediately after the war thousands of military-surplus machines were sold off at public auctions. Recently demobbed soldiers were desperately seeking their own transport, and as factories switched from war work to the business of making a profit in the new age, even aircraft makers turned their hand to creating new designs of motorcycle. There was a whole plethora of two-men-and-a-boy firms that produced lightweight machines for the masses. In Redruth there was such a person who reputedly made a few in a small garage in Clinton Road. It was called, naturally enough, The Clinton. No example of it survives today, not unexpectedly since only three were actually made. Firms such as AJS, Norton, Velocette and Rudge competed in the Isle of Man, and reaped huge rewards in terms of sales not only in this country, but also abroad.

Up to the late twenties there were still more motorcycles in various forms on Cornish roads than there were cars. Local garages employed men who had learned their trade in the war, and could turn their hands to most mechanical things. There had always been a strong engineering tradition in the County, and the need to attend to petrol-engined vehicles as opposed to the previous trade in steam or even horse drawn vehicles was obvious. Comleys Garage in St Austell

was one such establishment. Principally they dealt with motorcycles, and a gun dealership was also part of their small empire, but they were well able to cope with broken binders, push bikes and bent shovels

Percy Seward remembers: "We used to get in great big sidecar outfits that belonged to farmers. In many cases this would have been the first piece of mechanical equipment they had owned and as a result there was always plenty of work to do. For instance, the badly set up and maintained outfits were not always easy to control, and on many occasions they had been stopped by application of a stone hedge rather than by the brakes provided. We regularly ordered sets of forks from Birmingham, and I used to have to go up to St Austell Station and collect a bunch of brand new forks. This was quite a regular trade, we got through loads of not just forks but also all the other bits and pieces as well. If a machine came in with a puncture we might have a complete spare wheel with a good tyre, from an entirely different make of bike but which would fit. We put it in and the customer would drive off perfectly satisfied, not caring if his bike was made of bits from half a dozen different manufacturers as long as it got him home in time for milking."

Competitions amongst would-be racers were very popular in the twenties. Hill climbs were often staged on closed roads with a good gradient and smooth surface.

Herrbie Shear remembered "We had a hill climb at Little Polgooth once. Fiddler Mays Hill was closed, there was a policeman at the top and another at the bottom. A man called Rescorl won it on an AJS. I can still remember the noise, he had taken off his silencer, and also the smell of the oil he was using. He flew past me with his back wheel skidding all over the place."

A 1924 Norton 16H used to take a family out to the moors, (from the Heywood Collection.)

The near deserted streets of Bude in the early twenties make a stark contrast with today's traffic congestion. The Ariel motorcycle has a wicker sidecar which may indicate that its owner had sporting pretensions.

Brothers, Thomas Henry and Richard James(Jim) Hawken (riding pillion). This was at Zelah in the late twenties and shows a Rudge. Whilst riding this motorcycle Thomas had a serious accident and pierced his lung.

The Triumph sidecar outfit shows other members of the Hawken family at Zelah in 1927.

Above: The owner of this outfit was clearly more interested in his brand new plough than the daily transport parked by the cart shed. Taken near Greensplat, early twenties.

Right: A Royal Enfield at Gunnislake - the rider Clarence Murton.

THE MOTOR CYCLIST REVIEW — October, 1926

PREFERENCE

What's *your* preference? Single, twin, two-stroke, four-stroke, solo or sidecar?

Well, they have each got their merits, and to a great extent it depends upon you and what sort of service you want from the machine as to which is the most suitable for you.

That is where we are out to assist you. The buying of a motor cycle isn't like the purchase of a new tie or a new suit—the "How much is it? I'll have it" kind of buying. No! When WE sell a machine we like to talk the question over very carefully with our customer before we add to his existing preference our own recommendations as to what, in our opinion, will be the most suitable machine for him to buy.

..........and we'll stand or fall by our recommendations, too; we give a good AFTER-SALES service as well as a conscientious sales service, and are out to make every customer who comes into our establishment a customer for life—and also one who will never hesitate to recommend us to any of his friends interested in motor cycling.

BLIGHT'S GARAGE
STICKER, ST. AUSTELL
PHONE 128X5.

Printed for the Proprietors, T. G. SIMPSON & Co., LTD., Maxwell House, Arundel St., London, W.C.2, by Turner & Dunnett Ltd., London & Liverpool.

Fools Corner at Lanivet, from a painting by Geoffrey M Hough commissioned by Peter Old.

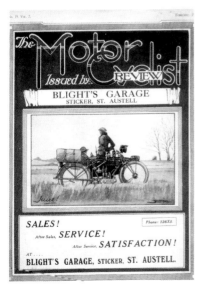

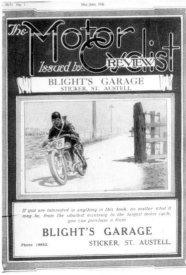

There must have been a good salesman around in 1927! Blights of Sticker was, and indeed still is, a small garage in a rural village near St Austell. Blights were appointed agents for OK Supreme Motorcycles, but then so was Sweets garage in Polgooth just a few miles away. We shall probably never know how many OK's they eventually sold.

Left: JAP engines were used by many manufacturers, this machine, which is unidentified, is one of the Heywood stable.

Below: 1922, Will and Gwennie Williams at Bojevans, Sancreed.

Above: These are the Richard sisters on their big Royal
Enfield in Falmouth about 1924

Left: A well dressed but anonymous gentleman near
Cury in the early twenties

THESE COMBINATIONS LOOK MUCH MORE ATTRACTIVE WHEN THE GIRLS ARE IN THEM!

Left: Reggie Harris was a cousin of Kenny Cock of Hughville Street, Camborne. The photograph of him on this early twenties big port AJS was taken near where the present Camborne Fire Station is. There used to be a First World War tank parked there as some kind of memorial. A similar tank was parked on The Green in Falmouth and they were both taken away for scrap during WW2.

A 1924 3$^{1}/_{2}$hp BSA Model S purchased new by Jimmy Ball from W. Foster and son of Polbathic. This BSA outfit eventually found its way back to its original owner's family. It has now been handsomely restored and is seen here at the West of England Steam Engine Show in 2004.

It was one of the dangers of older bikes. A bit too much advance on the magneto, flooded carburettor, a backfire which rapidly grows unless immediate action is taken. Earth and grass will not put out a petrol fire, and this Norton on fire at Manadon certainly attracted a crowd of onlookers.

A lightweight two-stroke or sidevalve was a utilitarian machine but served a purpose for everyday use, and was at least better than the push bike it replaced.

Left: Although many ladies rode at the time, this young lady was the pillion passenger and was just posing on this 1928 350cc James. Note the cushion on the rear carrier.
Below: The rider of this New Hudson pauses by the road near Saltash in the late twenties.

Left: Alan Wakeford at Truck Hill, Probus. The AJS is a 1927 sidevalve H9, but its difficult to tell if this is a new or contemporary shot.

Below: An ABC (All British Company) at a bridge around 1928 possibly Ruan Lanihorne.

Two more from the Heywood collection. Both ABC's, perhaps both parties wishing they were somewhere else. The one below was taken at St Ives station.

A Sunday afternoon outing to Mount Edgecumbe for the Johns family of Landrake.

A 1921 Wolf with a 550 JAP engine seen here at a farm near Egloskerry in the forties.

Left: Peter Sandry and his 6HP Douglas outfit at St Merryn

Below: Peter Old's 'stop me and buy one' ice cream sidecar. Once owned by the renowned Newlyn artist Charles Simpson who used it to carry his paints and easels. Peter now takes it to charity functions and on VMCC club runs, and still manages to dish out the ice creams from a hidden gas powered fridge inside the body of the sidecar.

Left: 1921 2^3/4 hp Douglas, similar to those used by dispatch riders in World War 1.
Below: This Quadrant was once owned by Jack Bacon of Tywardreath, who swapped a grandfather clock for it.

Taken at 8 Honey Street Bodmin, the motorcycle is a 1927 998cc V twin BSA. The man in the white coat is Mr Locke himself, and the other gentleman is Mr A J Hearn.

The Thirties and the Second World War

The early years of the thirties and the Depression was a trying time for the industry. Long established manufacturers were having to make short cuts which in many cases led to their eventual total demise or their amalgamation with other firms. Lightweight utility machines could be bought very cheaply brand new. A 98cc Excelsior for example was priced at £14.15.00. Conventional and larger capacity machines continued to be made, although in much smaller numbers. The car was now the preferred transport

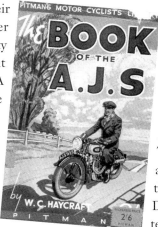

of the masses yet still there was a market for those who for reasons perhaps of economy or conservatism wanted two or three wheels to get them about.

There was a great deal of interest in sport and competition. At a national level people looked to Brooklands or the Isle of Man for their inspiration, whilst locally there was much to see and to take part in. Every Easter, near St Agnes, on a rough track on top of a steep cliff thousands gathered to watch as competitors in the Motorcycling Clubs Lands End Trial struggled to wrestle their bikes to the top without either stopping or putting their feet down. The riders had been up all night travelling from as far away as London, tackling hill after hill in an attempt to win a coveted Finishers Award. Blue Hills at St Agnes was the one that they all regarded as their nemesis. To fail or succeed in front of so many experts who gave willingly and noisily of their advice, opinion and encouragement was a daunting prospect for the fatigued entrants. But it also provided many a tale for the pub or the fireside long after the event was over. Ruses Mill, Crackington and Darracott were other well known Cornish hills in the Lands End Trial.

Elsewhere, for those more interested in speed, there were plenty of options. Grasstrack racing, and its cousin speedway, was a popular spectator event. At Falmouth the local club decided that in the late thirties there was a ready made mini Isle Of Man circuit right on their doorstep. The Pendennis Road Races, organised at the end of the thirties, used the road that went around Castle Drive by the Docks. Several well known aces were tempted from up country and took part in the event, but its closeness to the start of the war unfortunately curtailed further development and along with many other kinds of motor sport its operation was suspended for the duration.

Because there was very little real preparation for war most of the motorcycles used by the Forces were simply successful civilian models devoid of trimmings and painted matt khaki. Those supplied to the German Army were to be purpose-built for military service. Before the war had ended suggested designs for post war machines were already being discussed. These ranged from diesels to home assembly kits, streamliners to everyman commuters.

This BSA sports a fashionable launch bodied sidecar from the early thirties, photograph taken in Lanivet.

This early thirties Matchless shows all the design points of its time. The sporting look was created using high level exhausts, a sloping engine and the then new saddle tank. This machine belonged to Martin Northam of South Street St Austell. He used it during the Second World War to commute from his home to RAF St Eval, where he was employed as an aircraft technician.

Above: This garage stood on what is now The Capitol car park in St Austell.

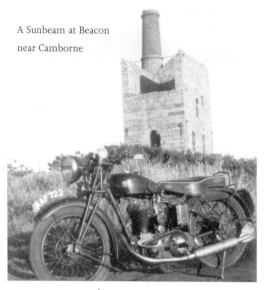

A Sunbeam at Beacon
near Camborne

Above: A pre war Triumph Tiger 70 that once belonged
to a District Nurse in the Bude area.

CORNISH NUMBER PLATES.

When registration numbers were first introduced in this Country each county was allocated a two letter prefix for its own exclusive use. Cornwall was given AF. At first both cars and motorcycles were given the same number, thus there were two AF 1'S on the road at the same time. AF 1 was a Benz car owned by Dr. Dowding of Newlyn East. AF 1 was also a two and three quarter horsepower BAT registered on the 7th of December 1903 to A.H.Gadson of Redhill in Surrey. This may simply have been a very early example of someone wishing to own a distinctive number plate, or maybe the gentleman had a home in both Surrey and Cornwall. The first motorcycle registered and apparently kept in Cornwall was AF 3 - a two and three quarter horse power Humber, new to G.F.Walker of Falmouth.

The AF series went to 1924, it was succeeded by RL which only lasted until 1928 when CV took over to take it to 1933. Thereafter the three letter prefix started with ACV, then ARL and finally with AAF. There are still many people who can date a vehicle from its registration number alone.

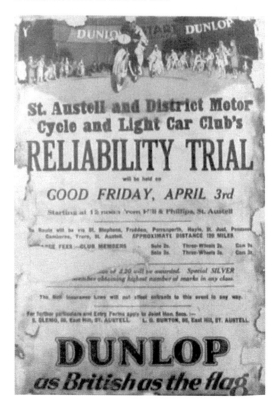

St. Austell and District Motor
Cycle and Light Car Club's

RELIABILITY TRIAL

will be held on

GOOD FRIDAY, APRIL 3rd

Starting at 12 noon from Hill & Phillips, St. Austell

DUNLOP
as British as the flag

Charlie and Marion Lucas went on a camping holiday to Looe during the summer of 1935. Their chosen transport was a unit construction New Imperial. The rest of the family had already arrived by train from Bristol.

Bob Collins was a well known grass tracker and a member of the Collins family motorcycle business in Truro. At the start of his career he rode a Dirt Track Douglas, pictured here near St Austell in the early thirties.

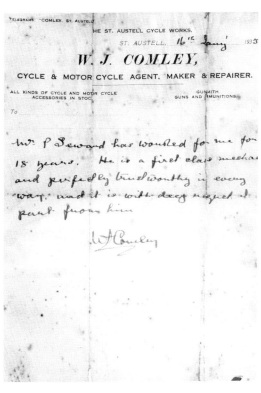

Above: A 1935 Douglas with Bob Collins just about to set off on a Lands End Trial.

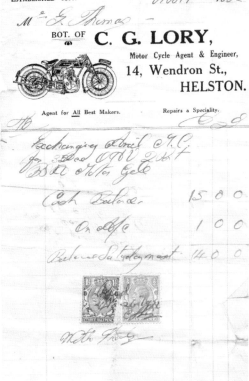

Previous page and above: The Seward family transport in the early thirties. The motive power, a 1929 500cc Raleigh, remained the same but the sidecar changed regularly.

Above: This rare 1929 500cc Humber was owned by the Hitchens family of Vanvean Farm, Polgooth

Below: This wartime shot of an unknown gentleman on his New Imperial was taken at Pothole near Sticker. Note the blackout mask on the headlight.

Left: George Rowley on the works 350cc Overhead Camshaft AJS. This is the machine he used in the Castle Drive races at Falmouth before the Second World War.

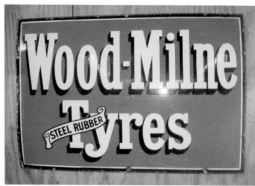

Left: The BSA Sloper was so named after its forward sloping engine

Below: An early driving licence belonging to Percy Seward

Nº 216501

Licence for One Motor Bicycle or Tricycle at £1:0:0.

*Percy Seward

of 1 Brewery Pce, in the

Civil Parish or Township of StAustell within the

Administrative County† of Cnll

is hereby authorized to keep ONE MOTOR BICYCLE or TRICYCLE, from the date hereof until the *31st day of December* next following; the sum of ONE POUND having been paid for this Licence.

Granted at StAustell

this 10th day of June 1920

by D Brutton

* NOTE—Name to be inserted in full.
†If the residence is within a County Borough strike out "Administrative" and insert "Borough" after "County".
S.D. 1919.

Above: The young Les Willis on a 1935 350cc side valve BSA

Below: Les Willis's uncle on a Rex-Acme Blackburne engined motorcycle in 1929

Above: The big Levis machines were often robbed of their engines which were fitted into home made grass track or speedway bikes.

Right: Amy Jenkins at Portscatho on a her Levis in 1932.

Martin Jennings on the Rudge he used for vintage racing

Ray Powell and Boo Cock pose with Ray's 1937 International Norton at Chiverton Cross Garage.

A group of riders pose outside Roses garage at St Andrews Road, Par. The top photograph was taken in 1927, the lower one some 60 years later in 1987 when the scene was re enacted by members of the Vintage Motor Cycle Club. The AJS at the extreme left is the same machine in both pictures. Both are historic photos now as Keith Pearce, the current owner, has replaced the old tin buildings with modern showrooms.

Left: An early Big Port AJS converted to a hill climber with later forks and other modifications. Originality came second to speed and reliability at that time.

Below: BSA not only made two-wheelers but also three wheeled cars like this one, driven by Julia Jennings of Camborne.

A BSA M20 on guard duty near Camelford just before D-Day.

A wartime Ariel, model W/NG, seen here just after the war and in snow at St Stephens.

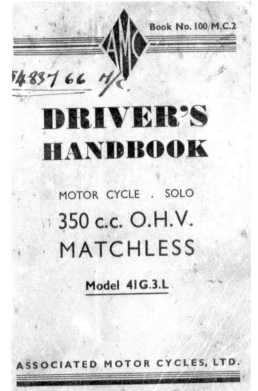

Above: A young Henry Prisk on a War Department Matchless in St Agnes.

A rider's handbook for a wartime Matchless. This was issued to 5483766 W E Rickeard, who was probably called up after the war because on the back of the accompanying booklet, in his own handwriting and amongst little reminders such as "drill in threes", he has written "20 weeks to go."

Koben Triggs works on a 1947 Triumph Speed Twin that once belonged to Aubrey Masters of Bodmin. Aubrey rescued the Triumph from a layby where it had been abandoned.

Post War and the Fifties

With the return of peace came the demand for newer improved models. Engines and other components were assembled once again into a variety of similar yet individualised makes. BSA, as part of its war reparations, had obtained a pre-war DKW design, and with only minor changes marketed it as the Bantam, one of the Birmingham firm's all time best sellers. In a process reminiscent of forty years earlier, an army of small lightweights such as Norman, Francis-Barnett, and Excelsior took to the streets. British factories produced machines that were exported all over the world, sometimes at the expense of the home market.

A curious design, which, had always been around, was the clip-on. This was a small engine that could be attached to an ordinary push bike, giving immediate motive power. These little engines could be, just as in the pioneer years, hung on to the frame, put in the rear wheel or even attached to the handlebars. The agricultural engineering firm of Teagles, whose family run factory is still situated near Blackwater, decided to cash in on this market. They had a small two-stroke engine of their own design which they used to power grain elevators, hedge trimmers and the like. They adapted this motor such that it fitted a bicycle immediately behind the saddle, with roller rubbing on the rear tyre. The whole thing was raised or lowered according to need, and a throttle on the handlebar controlled the speed. Of its type, this was quite a successful design, and was really the only volume produced motorcycle, or very close relative at least, ever made in Cornwall.

New designs were victorious in all kinds of competitions, and names such as Triumph, Norton, AJS and Matchless became synonymous with a quality product in overseas markets.

In Cornwall there was still much activity on the competition scene. Trengwainton House near Penzance was the home of a popular hill climb event, and road racing was going on at Camelford and St Eval. Scrambles, grasstracks and trials were much in evidence at weekends, with the County providing some extremely capable riders, some of whom got to national level. There was a long established speedway track at Par Stadium, where peculiar left handed banked sidecars diced with each other, skilfully handled at the hands of such people as Phil Williams, Roy Wedlake and Dave and Ken Westaway.

But by the end of the decade the British motorcycle industry had become complacent. There were signs that the sales success enjoyed in previous years was being seriously challenged. The industry had failed to invest sufficiently in new engineering and design technology and had also failed to recognise the change in public demand.

Brian Lobb remembers: "I worked in a motorcycle shop in mid-Cornwall. I am not going to tell you which one because the owner is still around and it rankles even to this day! One Saturday, just before we were going to close for the weekend a young chap came in pushing a BSA Gold Star. Now that was a very desirable bike then, as it still is now. He told us that he had been down here

on holiday and the bike had broken. He had to get back up country to start work on the following Monday morning, he knew we were just closing and probably wouldn't be able to fix the bike, but were we interested in doing a part exchange deal on one of the Triumphs we had in the shop? The boss was always ready to make money, and eventually he gave the chap a good discount in exchange for the broken down Goldie, as well as a small amount of cash. Off rode the man and his Triumph, and we began to thoroughly examine the bike. It was in really good condition, which is why we accepted it in the first place, good compression, fat blue spark, timed correctly, valves OK. Yet nothing we did would persuade the thing to start. We put it in the workshop until our ace mechanic could have a proper look at it.

Monday morning came and our specialist knowledge and combined brute strength still couldn't make it run. 'We are going to have to take the head off and look inside. Off came the cylinder head bolts and up popped the head into the air. Inside, where a piston should have been was a tightly coiled bed spring, providing all the compression in the world!

Kenny Cock pictured at Foundry Square, Hayle in 1947. The bike is a 1930 BSA Sloper. information (left) on the photograph provided by Boo Cock.

52

This is Rocky Park near St Austell in 1948, and it shows Bob Collins on his JAP. Later that year, Bob was killed whilst riding here on the same bike. He was one of the top riders in the country. Grass Track racing in Cornwall was halted for a long while after this incident in Cornwall.

Bob Collins leads Ivan Kessell in this dusty scene at Treviscoe in 1946.

Below: A Villiers Starmaker powered grass track bike pictured at a meeting in 1959.

Above: 1951 and these two St Austell boys have just been called up for National Service. They are enjoying the last days of civilian freedom on their nearly new machines.
Left: A beach scene at Porthpean in 1951.

Left: This is a Corgi, developed from the wartime paratroopers' Wellbike, here ridden by young Mark Seward.

Below: This Norton 16H in full weatherproof kit was for the ride to work end of the market.

Above: St Austell Gulls speedway team in 1951 in their match against the Americans. Jack Luke (right) oversees.

Below: Mick Mitchell demonstrates the leg trailing style of speedway at Par Stadium in 1952.

Ally Clift and Colin Dommett pose in 1958 at the back of Smokey Joes cafe near Scorrier. The bike is an ACS, a Tandon based special that Ally built himself.

Des Harris and Ally Clift at Blackwater in 1954, scrambling in every sense of the word.

Left: This Enfield Model G belonged to Alfie Pellow of St Erth, who was the local barber. The lady is his sister Joan Rod, the little boy is Terry Rod. Date is around 1951.

Below: The signs on the shed indicate that this is Richard Moyles' Nursery in Redruth in 1955.

The Teagle was just about the only two wheeler manufactured in Cornwall, although it was not a true motorcycle. It was a 50cc engine that had been adapted from a power unit designed originally for a hedge trimmer. Many thousands of these little motors were made from 1952 to 1964, and the normal daily output was just over 100 a day. It was eventually used in a motor scythe, lawn mower, motor cultivator and as in this instance a power pack on a standard bicycle. The motor ran a pulley that was raised or lowered onto the rear tyre as required. The engine is shown fitted to a bicycle in Charlie Williams collection. The gentleman seen operating the hedge trimmer is one of the Teagle Family.

60

Nancemellin, 1963, and Jeff Smith on a works 420cc BSA leads Adrian Kessel on a 350cc JAP, and Ally Clift on his 500cc ACS. John Tribble is in the background, John Bassett wears the white armband.

Taken at a test day on Perranporth Aerodrome, this shows the Triumph that Ken Brough rode in a Clubmans TT. Ken was a quiet man who had worked in the research and development department at BSA. That day all riders got a "ton" out of the machine.

Cyril Furse delivered milk to the residents of the steep back roads of Mevagissey for many years. He lived on a farm at the top of School Hill, and used a variety of Nortons as the motive power source for the sidecar, which was made for him by Bob Barron.

Cyril Furse's sidecar still exists, it is attached here to a 1921 800cc V twin AJS.

The mobylette, a popular and cheap form of mass transport.

Another Mevagissey machine rescued minutes before it was going to be buried. Some might say this late forties James autocycle should have been interred, but it is probably just restorable.

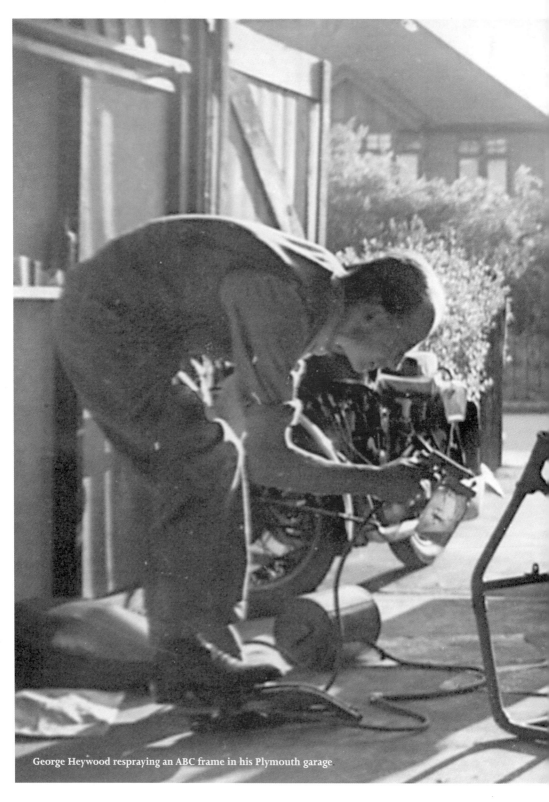

George Heywood respraying an ABC frame in his Plymouth garage.

Fiddling with a Scott, two-strokes again!

"I paid £50 for this Vincent in 1959 which was a lot of
money then, I was on about £12 a week at the time."
John Rowse, Saltash.

"Ok, but it's not as good as the one I had before the war, now that would go!. Anyway the rigid ones handled better than these new rear sprung bikes. And another thing…."

Above: Joan and Tony Goldsworthy of Fourlanes on his Triumph Thunderbird 650cc taken at Treskillard near Redruth around 1955.

Below: The Thunderbird is joined by a BSA.

Before and after shots. This ex-Post Office rigid Bantam was owned by Charlie Williams of Redruth. It was purchased and sent to America where Brian Slark of the Barber Museum quickly and expertly converted it to a replica trials machine. It was then presented to Irene, the wife of Jeff Smith as a retirement present for all the work she had done for AHRMA, the American Historic Racing Motorcycle Association. Irene was the sister of John Draper, and the little Bantam was her first bike. She rode it very succesfully in the Cotswolds trials.

A Norton nonchalantly leaning against a tree at Par stadium., whilst the owner has gone off to watch the speedway. There is something a bit special about this bike; it has an International engine and other improvements such as an alloy tank, air scoop in the front brake and lightened parts. When testers first rode this model they likened the handling to a ride on a feather bed. Nortons from then on were known for their 'featherbed' frames.

A 1947 350 overhead camshaft KSS Velocette belonging to Les Willis of St Austell.

THE SIXTIES

By around 1960 the popularity of the German NSU and the French Mobylette moped had brought about the demise of the British industry in the market. This was followed by the Italian, Vespa and Lambretta scooter invasion. The designer Alec Issigonis and his 850cc Mini conspired to take another great chunk out of the British motorcycle industry. And Japan was happening.

Honda's success was based on the fact that they did not rest on their laurels, as had the British. Slowly, as a result of competition and continuous development and alongside Yamaha and Suzuki, they began to dominate the world lightweight motorcycle market. The writing was on the wall for home based manufacturers who had contrived to make reliable yet largely old fashioned machines. Although Cornwall was not much disturbed by the Mods and Rocker rivalry, the image of motorcycling was not well presented to the public at large By the end of the decade the British motorcycle was practically non existent. Those that remained would linger on

for a few more years before they too succumbed to the inevitable. If you were going to buy a decent bike, be it big or small, you would have to buy it from a firm based either on the Continent or in Japan.

John Milton remembers: "One of the gang I used to go around with had a Cotton which we really liked. We put it up against a new 100cc Suzuki, the idea being to see which one would go up Pentewan Hill the best. The Cotton pulled away from the bottom but when it had to restart on the steep bend half way up both the engine and the clutch protested noisily, as did the owner who had to try and hold it upright whilst having a car right up his backside.

The little Suzuki which was light and extremely buzzy and had a funny toe and heel foot change on the wrong side smoked, but easily outperformed the British bike. We didn't want this to happen, but had to grudgingly admit that it was quite a good little bike for a 100cc thing, and after all the Japs couldn't build big bikes like our Triumphs could they?"

A 1960 BSA Super Rocket at Carnmoggas, Little Polgooth in 1969. This bike once did Bristol to Shrewsbury on a Saturday morning in less time than Tony Blackburn took to do 'Junior Choice' on the radio. That is, under 2 hours.

The highest point in Cornwall, Brown Willy, conquered by a Lambretta in 1963

Left: The Vincent and engine house, Condurrow.

Above: Jim Jennings was also able to tune a pretty mean road going machine.

Below: Martin Jennings at Portreath on his Triumph engined Puissant.

Alan Wakeford's 350 Gold Star suffers from wheelspin as he tries to get up a section in a Camel Vale Trial near Par.

Above: Ariel engines waiting to be fitted to frames.

Left: A collection of timing covers make a nice wall decoration in Tom Seward's workshop.

Tom Seward discusses one of his Ariels with Roger Fogg.

This Ariel, with an appropriate registration number, was once owned by David Paull of Blackwater.

The Japanese manufacturers introduced small but sophisticated products in the early sixties. It was the beginning of the end for the British motorcycle industry.

Jim Jennings doesn't quite make the corner on his big Vincent at Trengwainton Hill Climb near Penzance.

Above: Along with Tigers' tails and hanging things from the end of the handlebars it was deemed the height of fashion to have a plastic tiger skin seat cover on the bike in the sixties.

Left: This rider at Penzance is using a wartime dispatch rider's coat and leggings to keep out the rain sweeping in across Mounts Bay.

79

A small fin BB34 Gold Star registration SCV 650 in the hands of Alan Wakeford in the rain at Mallory Park road races

CORNWALL CENTRE OF THE AUTO-CYCLE UNION

SUPPLEMENTARY REGULATIONS FOR AN OPEN TO CENTRE ROAD RACE MEETING FOR SOLO

MOTOR CYCLES & THREE WHEELERS

HELD UNDER THE STANDING REGULATIONS, 1966 EDITION AND 10TH EDITION GENERAL COMPETITION RULES OF THE ACU., TOGETHER WITH THESE SUPPLEMENTARY REGULATIONS.

ACU PERMIT No.   TCC No. 548

SUNDAY 24TH AUGUST 1969 AT THE ST.EVAL AIRFIELD CIRCUIT, NR.NEWQUAY, CORNWALL

PRACTISING 0930 - 1030 HRS   RACING TO START AT 1200 HRS

1.   OFFICIALS

CENTRE STEWARDS:-   A.HORE. E.J.COLLINS.
(APPOINTED BY CORNWALL CENTRE)
CLERK OF THE COURSE:-   M.S.WILLIAMS.
ASSISTANT:-   W.A.WHITE.
CHIEF SCRUTINEER:-   R.H.L.DAVEY.
FINISH OF RACE RECORDER:-   MRS.B.JONES.
JUDGE:-   W.MARTIN.
SECRETARY OF THE MEETING:-   B.H.JERMEY, 14, QUARRY PARK TERRACE,
                               BODMIN, CORNWALL.
                               TEL: BODMIN 2420.

2.   ELIGIBILITY TO BE ELIGIBLE TO ENTER THIS COMPETITION DRIVERS MUST BE REGISTERED MEMBERS OF A CLUB IN THE CORNWALL CENTRE. APPLICATIONS FOR MEMBERSHIP OF A CLUB IN THE CORNWALL CENTRE MAY BE SENT TO THE SECRETARY OF THE MEETING BY 2ND AUGUST 1969., WITH A FEE OF 10/-.

3.   ENTRIES   CLOSING DATE FOR ENTRIES IS 12 NOON ON 2ND AUGUST 1969.

ENTRY FEES:-

SOLOS - £2 FOR ONE EVENT AND £1 FOR EACH ADDITIONAL EVENT.
THREEWHEELERS - £3 FOR ONE EVENT AND £1 FOR EACH ADDITIONAL EVENT.
    THE PROMOTERS WILL PAY DRIVERS PERSONAL ACCIDENT AND THIRD PARTY INSURANCE.
    ENTRY FEES WILL ONLY BE RETURNED IF THE MEETING IS CANCELLED OR POSTPONED FOR MORE THAN 24 HOURS.

4.   LIMITATION OF ENTRIES ENTRIES WILL BE LIMITED TO THE NUMBERS SHOWN IN PARA. 5.

5.   EVENTS ENTRIES WILL BE ACCEPTED OF MACHINES IN CATEGORY A1 SOLO AND CATEGORY B1, B2, THREEWHEELER IN THE CLASSES LISTED UNDER:-

| | | LAPS | | MAX | MAX |
| | | | | ENTRY | FEE |
		HEAT	FINAL		RACE
EVENT 1	OVER 100cc NOT OVER 125cc SOLOS.	6	8	25	25
EVENT 2	OVER 125cc NOT OVER 250cc SOLOS.	6	8	50	25
EVENT 3	OVER 250cc NOT OVER 350cc SOLOS.	6	8	50	25
EVENT 4	OVER 350cc NOT OVER 1300cc SOLOS.	6	8	50	25
EVENT 5	OVER 100cc NOT OVER 1300cc SOLOS.	6	8	100	25
EVENT 6	THREEWHEELERS NOT OVER 1300cc	6	8	24	12

Above: A monocoque framed Triumph built for racing in Redruth by Malcolm Watson, outside the now demolished hangar at St Eval.

Left: St Eval Airfield was the venue for a series of motorcycle races in the sixties. These regulations from Cornwall Centre ACU are a reminder of names associated with these events.

Above: Martin Jennings with a racing Triumph and **below** on an early TZ Yamaha racer.

Above: A 250cc Tiger Cub with fairing and all the goodies.

Above, left and next page: Typical of the machines that raced at St Eval, included here are a Triumph Bonneville, a Norvin, a Sprayson special and a Triton.

The Mod craze came to Cornwall, as shown by this much illuminated Vespa in the sixties.

The 173cc Sachs-engined (left) Progress scooter was made in Germany and was a very rare sighting in one of the MCC Trials in North Cornwall unlike the Lambretta (right) which was more common.

Above: This down at heel Durkopp Diana obviously needs some work. **Right:** A Moto Rumi scooter ridden by Eileen Ferguson of Cannons Town at Chiverton Cross. **Below:** Leah and Tara learn to ride on a Honda 50 in a nice safe field in Lanjeth. Dad showing them how to do it properly on the same bike fell heavily and suffered more from pride than the collar bone injuries.

Jim Jennings of Camborne was for many years associated with Vincents and built up quite a reputation for knowing how to put them together properly. There was scarcely a Vincent in the County that he had not worked on, and here are some of them outside his workshop. In his younger years, Jim had known Lawrence of Arabia.

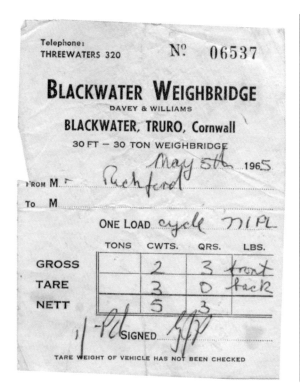

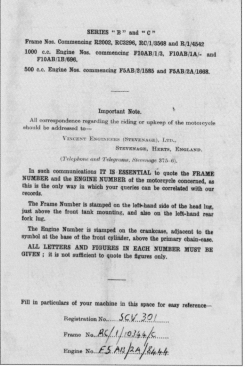

Graham Richford made sure the documentation on his Vincent was filled out correctly.

Mike Jenkins' very original 1954 Triumph was owned by Edward Freethy, who rode it 97,226 miles whilst on his daily journey to work from Michaelstow to Padstow. Mike continues to use it and has done several eventful trips abroad on this normally reliable machine.

Mervyn Pearces Matchless on the Bodmin bypass.

This fine AJS outfit belongs to Barry Stephens of St Just.

Brian Hooley's 1960 alternator equipped 350cc Matchless.

Adam Faith and the Roulettes came to the City Hall in Truro in 1960, and took part in a charity raffle. The prize was a new Lambretta scooter, registered 1 UAF, the same as the popstar's initials. Shaking hands are W.H.Collins of Collins Motorcycles in Truro, looking on is Kingsley Smith of Criddle and Smith. Photo courtesy Tom and Robert Roskrow.

Doc Kitt's rigid G3 Matchless.

Above: An Electra Glide in Looe.

Below: Julia Jennings and friend with a Vincent Black Shadow.

Harry Ross of Bodmin on a 500cc Velocette Clubman in 1968.

Polgooth's Pat Clancy on a pre-war MAC Velocette in 1973.

A sectioned Douglas as exhibited on the factory stand now owned by Charlie Williams.

Phil Williams of Tywardreath raced a variety of fast, well prepared sidecar outfits.

Lloyd Watson of Redruth and his son David make adjustments to this racing Cotton JAP at Silverstone during one of the MCC's High Speed trials.

An early Honda Gold Wing near Camelford.

Curly Hunt and a Triumph Bonneville named Tokyo Rose near Minions on Bodmin Moor.

Olly Lamper of Bodmin on his way to support John Deacon at the French ISDE. This overloaded 1975 XT500 was ridden there all in one go, but Olly had to put talcum powder down his trousers.

A 1972 Norton Commando Roadster, at a lock up in Bodmin.

Sally Madgwick, long time activist with Camel Vale MCC and The Trail Riders Fellowship pictured with her 1980 Suzuki GS750, in 1980.

1975 Moto Morini Strada 350. This bike owned by Sally Madgwick and nicknamed 'Lil Red Rooster.'

Above: A 1978 MV Agusta 350cc Ipotesti belonging to Stan Weston of Newlyn East. Ipotesti is Italian for hypothesis.

Below: A chopper based on a Triumph Trident belonging to Curly Hunt, nicknamed Tumblin' Dice.

Tokyo Rose, the chopped Bonneville, takes its place in the front room of a house in Bodmin.

Sammy Miller encourages a group of youngsters at Trethurgy in 1977.

The very young Mark Seward on his second bike, a little Suzuki.

Phil Farrar shows off the cup he won at a Cubert Show in 1980 for the restoration of this Ariel Square four'.

The Cat. Dave Saunby's lovely Triton at a Pendennis show around 1985.

Sally Madgwick's Triton waiting to be hill climbed at Porthkerris in1988. It had a wideline featherbed frame with a T110 motor, The clip-ons did not help on the twisty track at all.

A 1978 Suzuki GS 750 in a ford at Clerkenwater. Modifications to this bike included racy yellow paint and a lightweight drilled plastic chain guard.

Above: Dave Howells, Maico, Cornwall Scramble Club meeting near Mitchell 1978.

Left: Same bike, same rider, near Kit Hill, Callington four years earlier.

Above: Michael Curnow of Redruth with the Flashman Trophy after winning at Cornwall Scrambling Club's meeting at Hendra Farm, MItchell in 1981.

Left: Gary Prisk on his 1976 250cc Bultaco Sherpa at Wheal Kitty St Agnes.
Below: Gary showing how to get out of a traffic jam.

Above: The winning South West Team at Cornwall Scramble Club's Motocross in 1979.

Left to Right: Mike Curnow, Les Coombe, Dave Wills, Patrick Mitchell, Alan Evans and Ross Frazer.

A Rickman Triumph belonging to Neil Browne at Porthkerris in 1988.

Bodmin Boghoppers met at Smiths Garage in Bodmin every Sunday to ride over the moors. This picture shows them in 1986. Left to right; Dave Hearn, George Martin, Olly Lamper, Colin and Mrs George, Kevin Hull and founder Mike Hull.

Five 1970's TS Suzuki's line up at Halgavor House in Bodmin ready for the day's ride.

Above: The future stars of the Isle of Man always start somewhere. Here in Rosenannon are friends Alan Bennallick on the 125cc Yamaha AS3, Puffer on a Honda CG125 and Derek on a CD175.

Below: Grass track racing at St Erme in 1985. Leading Alan Chapman is Claude Bennett on his BSA B25 special.

Camborne-Redruth Motor Club

SCRAMBLE

open to Cornwall Centre and held under the G.C.R. of the A.C.U

at Nancemellin, Camborne

on Sunday, 15th August

START 2.30 p.m.

Marshals, lap scorers and girls on the gate
are all members and friends of the C.R.M.C.

A.C.U. Steward — Mr. S. Williams
Club Stewards — Mr. A. Hore, Mr. B. Jennings
Pit Steward — Mr. M. Roberts
Starter — Mr. W. J. Martin
Clerk of the Course — Mr. R. Lawry
Secretary of the Meeting — Mr. M. Youlton

Warning . . . MOTOR RACING IS DANGEROUS

You are present at this meeting entirely at your own risk, and you are admitted subject to the conditions that all persons having connection with the promotion and organisation or conduct of this meeting, including the owners of all land and drivers and owners of the vehicles, are absolved from all liability in respect of personal injury whether fatal or otherwise to you, or damage to your property howsoever caused.

The organisers wish to thank those who have helped to run this meeting, especially the St. John Ambulance personnel and Mr. Olds and Mr. Bowden for the use of their land.

PENDENNIS MOTOR CYCLE CLUB
MOTOR CYCLE

GRASS TRACK RACING

at
POLLAWYN FARM QUINTRELL, NEWQUAY

on SUNDAY, 8th JUNE, 1975

at 2 p.m.

PERMIT APPLIED FOR

OFFICIALS:—

A.C.U. Steward — M. Roberts
Club Stewards — A. Green & A. Williams
Clerks of Course — M. Tremayne & E. Bray
Scrutineer — M. Greaney
Pit Marshals — S. & T. Pooley
Lap Scorers — D. Bostock & G. Chard
Chief Marshal — H. Rule
Starter — K. Pooley
Commentator — P. Warr
Gate Stewards — Ladies Committee
Sec. of Meeting — A. Green, 'Homeleigh', Treleiver Rd., Mabe, Penryn

Warning MOTOR CYCLE RACING IS DANGEROUS

You are present at this meeting entirely at your own risk and you are admitted subject to the conditions that all persons having connection with the promotion and organisation or conduct of this meeting, including the owners of all land and drivers and owners of the vehicles, are absolved from all liability in respect of personal injury whether fatal or otherwise to you, or damage to your property howsoever caused.

Please Do Not Cross The Track During Racing

Programme including admission 35p. Children & O.A.P.'s 10p

That was a five! A marshall retrieves a competitor's Yamaha from a tree at the top of Phils Find in an End to End trial.

Above: A BSA with a Triumph engine, a fine Tribsa built by Olly Lamper.

Below: A novel way to transport a hill climb bike. This MZ was photographed at Porthkerris.

Left: Adam Hillier on an MTX 125 with his mate Antony Devito in the early eighties at Porthtowan.
Below Left: Louise Hillier's first bike, a DT50. She was knocked off by a car, blew it up twice and was glad to get rid of it.
Below: Sally Madgwick on her 1975 Suzuki TS 125A. She still owns it.

Above: Margaret Ross on the R80RT BMW that was her daily transport from home in Bodmin to work in Padstow.

Below: The Moors Velocette Owners Club run in 1976. Harry Ross owns the BMW, the MNK registerd Velocette standing near Gerald Merchant later went to Japan.

Laft: Tony Powell, ferret handler and raconteur, seen at the counter of his shop in Camelford.

Below: Camelford Bike Bits, a mecca for those who need spare bits and pieces for their old machines, is owned by Tony Powell. An S7 Sunbeam is parked on the double yellow lines outside the shop.

Above: Charlie Williams explains things...
Left: A drawing of a BSA A65 by Martin Jennings in one of his school books, dating from the mid sixties.

Round the back of Penzance there was a garage full of old bikes that belonged to a man called Mr Prowse. He was a long time dealer, but as he got older the roof of the shed where he kept his collection began to give way. The bikes were stacked sometimes two or three high and there was a great variety of interesting but rusting relics in there. Although eventually some of them were retained locally, most were bought up by a dealer and taken out of the County.

Everyone's got a shed, and a bench.

Peter Old adjusts his gearchange lever.

Ian Thompson has problems with the CDI unit on an XT 250.

Doc Kitts retrieves a Penguin from his crib bag.

Roger Fogg tunes the carb with a shifting spanner.

Above: Paul Sowden of St Agnes tunes his Triumph

Below: A Honda Monkey bike in the woods near Duloe

Above: Louise Hillier at Malpas, Truro on an RD 350.

Below: A race tuned cousin of the above, an LC 250 Yamaha.

Participants riding past a marshall on The Martin Jennings Memorial Run at Tregrehan. Martin, who was from Camborne, was killed whilst racing in the Isle of Man.

Richard Dennison on the Guzzi and his mate on the Honda start from St Austell on a Grand European tour in 1990.

A Reliant-based special on its way to Cornwall pauses at Whiddon Down services in1996.

THE PRESENT

Idealists in the latter part of the twentieth century tried new innovations. Hub centre steering, monocoque chassis, rotary engines and feet first layouts were all tried out. But the motorcycle market had changed yet again. A bike is still a good way to get to work, but it is also a prestige plaything - a leisure pursuit like a small boat or a new surfboard. Modern manufacturers do not just go for practicalities in their designs, they go for image. Harley-Davison has been reborn thanks to careful marketing; similarly Triumph and BMW offer products which have much to do with the born again biker. The generation of baby boomers are now in a position where they have disposable income and are willing to spend it on toys such as motorcycles. Triumph of course has risen from the ashes, and under the ownership of John Bloor, whose main interest is property development, have created a new design and are selling very well at home and overseas.

The competition element in Cornwall is still strong. A speedway track has opened at Nanpean near St Austell, the former track near Par having been sold to provide the site for an indoor market.. It is the home of The St Austell Gulls and has a loyal following each Tuesday evening during the summer months. Trials, enduro, motocross, touring, road racing, greenlaning, commuting, collecting; they all have their champions and an army of followers, all riding motorcycles. The motorcycle is alive and very much kicking in Cornwall.

ST. AUSTELL SPEEDWAY

£1.00

MEETING NUMBER 91

ST. BLAZEY MOTORCYCLES ARE PLEASED TO SUPPORT THE GULLS

BRITISH SPEEDWAY
AMATEUR LEAGUE
ST. AUSTELL GULLS
v
EXETER/NEWPORT
WESTERN WARRIORS
Tuesday 3rd June 1997
at 7.30 p.m.

Above: The track was in a disused claypit near Old Pound. At the time of writing this has now been closed, and a new home for The Gulls has yet to be found.

Left: Programme number one of the newly revived St Austell Speedway.

Susan Pearce on a Harley Sportster in Polzeath.

Mean, Moody, Magnificent. John McMahon on his Harley at Pencalenick near Truro.

The fate of this little Victoria hangs in the balance at an auction. It has probably already been stripped of its original registration number which would have been transferred to a modern car. It was sold for £60.

There are some remarkable engineers in Cornwall, and Lloyd Watson is one of them. Being interested in owning a veteran bike, yet not finding one that he liked, Lloyd decided to build a brand new one from scratch. The barrels and head are of his own design though loosely based on Ariel castings, whilst the crankcase is all his own work. Frame and tank are home made, forks are original Druids. The magneto and carburettor all stem from before the First World War. With its Honda clutch and belt drive this remarkable machine would top 60 mph. LMC stands for Lloyds Motor Cycle. It now lives in a pub museum in London.

Matthew and Lisa Prisk (above) Katie (below right) and Bradley (below left) Maddever followed in their father's wheel tracks from a very young age.

Above: The motorcycle is easily the best way of passing slower traffic on narrow roads or in villages. Ladock, summer of 2004.

Below: Suzuki Intruder at Kit Hill Cafe in June 2004.

Above: A very far gone Louise Hillier as she rides a restored Henley in the Banbury Run. Despite the clutch cable disintegrating and the valve cap blowing out and the top of the carburettor float chamber falling off, victory ensued and Loo managed the finish, to much applause from her Dad.

Right: A very far gone Henley in the centre of the pile. The bike was made in Birmingham and had a 550cc Blackburne engine.

Above: A line up of learner machines outside Damerells of Whitemoor.

Below: The instructor's Honda with radio communication for the learners.

Above: Kate Sicolo poses on a Piaggio scooter, her daily transport to work in Truro.

Below: Tom Franks riding pillion for Sam in Perranporth and going through a phase in life. All the learner bikes belonging to their group of friends have now been replaced with bigger bikes or cars.

The Cornish team at the 1993 ISDE in Holland. Mark Seward, Tony Dinham and Julian Oates are the riders, Olly Lamper is team Coach. All three finished, and they were the second best club team. There were 600 starters, less than 100 finished.

Mark Seward scrambling on his much modified BSA Victor at Polawyn Farm, Fraddon in 1998.

For a few years a series of motocross meetings were held on the cliffs at Porthpean, with Crinnis as a background the course had spectacular views.

With Bishops Rock Lighthouse in the background this could hardly be anywhere else but the end of The Lands End Trial. Alan Keat driving.

Above: Mark Seward and Simon Rogers in their usual position in front of the pack at Weston Beach Races.

Left: Father Christmas arrives at Pencalenick School on a Metisse Outfit.

The old looking but only four-year-old Russian Ural outfit with Mignon Fogg in the very comfortable sidecar at Blackpool Pit near St Austell. This is the one that can reverse into pub car parks.

Above: The famous section up the side of the cliffs at Trevellas near St Agnes, known as Blue Hills, is owned by the Motor Cycling Club. It is gated and locked, only being opened twice a year, once for the Cornwall Centre ACU's End to End Trial, then again for the Lands End Trial proper.

Below: Alan Wakeford and his Velocette prepared for hill climbs, this is Hartland Quay and Alan was up against Ian Mitchell his friend annd rival.

Roger Maddever makes it to
the top of Blue Hills to win
the Lands End Trial in 1983.
Bike is a Yamaha XT250

Phil Farrar and his son Tom pose on their Triumph at the Tea Rooms on Kit Hill. Contrast this with the earlier pictures of Triumph motorcycles and their pillions.

Mac Services in Bodmin, noted for having half a motorcycle sticking out of the wall above the shop window, as well as for its friendly service.

Mervyn Pearce's retro bike at Polzeath the Kawasaki W650 that wants to be a Triumph Bonneville.

Above: The Cornwall Section of the Vintage Motorcycle Club gather at St Merryn airfield in 2003 for a flat tank experience. This involved members experiencing the joys of riding pre 1930 machines on private roads

The Army still has a use for dispatch riders. This group from the Territorial Army with military Armstrongs are doing navigation practice on Bodmin Moor. The motorcycle is now one of the only vehicles used by the Armed Services that still relies on petrol rather than diesel. Developmental work is going on to try and remedy this situation.

Above: David Hill of Nanstallon owns this three wheeler. The controls of the Messcherschmitt are similar to those of an aircraft. **Below:** Del Boy's family are alive and well have moved to Bugle, and are filling up at the roundabout garage in St Austell.

Before and after. Les Willis's restoration of this 1931 Ariel shows just how good he is at this painstaking work.

Above: The "Blackheads" outside the Driftwood Spars Hotel at St Agnes in the autumn of 2004. Many who are interested in particular aspects of motorcycling form clubs and groups to seek like minded souls. Thus, for example, you can join the Douglas Owners Club, The Trail Riders Fellowship, The South West Riders or The Swampdogs. The Blackheads, who are interested in road riding rather than a particular type of motorcycle meet each week for a ride, and often end up back at the pub in St Agnes.

Below: The 2004 Mega Run. Thousands of motorcycles from all over the South West converge on Plymouth Hoe for their annual Charity run.

Above: Dealers are not the only place you can buy a Fire Blade, this is a roadside plot near Roche.

Below: Netley Marsh Autojumble and Cornish left overs on offer at bargain prices.

Above: Ted Barrett's world travelling BSA M21.

Below: The Moscow trip. Cornish participants include Ted Barrett (1939 BSA), Peter Old (1937 BSA V-Twin) and Mick Glossop (1953 Velocette) pictured in 1991 at the start of the journey. Entitled "Once around Red Square and back." They rode all the way there, and all the way back.

Above: The final stretch into Red Square.

Below: Ted Barrett, Peter Old and Mick Glossop, all from Cornwall.

Ian Thompson of Newquay asks directions whilst visiting Brittany on his XT250.

If you are going to ride an ancient AJS all the way from Cornwall to the Somme Battlefields, it is probably better not to place old shells and grenades that you may find on the petrol tank. Time taken 8 days, St Austell to the Somme and back on a 65 year old motorcycle.

A Norton Commando Roadster on Route 66 in Missouri, just prior to repatriation to Truro.

The author riding a Cornish registered Kawasaki KLE 500 on the long wet road to the North Cape of Norway, somewhere above the Arctic Circle.

Tiffany Coates, based in Treen near Lands End, travels the world on her BMW called Thelma. This trip in 2001 was from Alaska to Tierra del Fuego at the tip of South America. These images from the journey typify the highs and lows of the committed long distance motorcycle traveller..

145

Cornish bikes in other countries. Louise Hillier and Gary Prisk gave up work for six months, bought a pair of Honda Dominators and shipped them across the Atlantic. The shots on these pages give an idea of their 24,000 mile journey from Nova Scotia down to Guatamala.

Death Valley, USA

Nexpa, Mexico

Kettle Valley, Canada

Guatemala

Above: Phil Farrar of Saltash- Triumph and Mont Blanc in 2004.

Below: Cornish bikes north of the Border. Peter Old's gold flash on the border.

Above: Gary Prisk tries to beg money from the local children with companions John Walker and Roger Madhatter.

St Agnes man Gary Prisk on his Honda Dominator NX 650 in Morroco.

Like Mr Webster's dictionary, we're Morroco bound. The Harley ridden by Roger Maddever parks next to a signpost that shows the way to Timbuctou.

Picture supplied by Pinnacle Photography www.ppauk.com

Whilst Art Editor of Cornish produced magazine Motorcycle Sport and Leisure in 2001, Louise Hillier trained with The Royal Signals White Helmets and jumped through fire on a Honda XR 250.

Richard Stevens of St Wenn had an adventurous life, and was always a motorcyclist at heart. He took over the ailing magazine that was then known as Motorcycle Sport from its owner Cyril Ayton and breathed new life into it. Mixing well known and much respected names from the world of motorcycles with local talent, he moulded the magazine under the leadership of its editor Peter Henshaw into what was probably the best magazine of the day. Richard was killed whilst riding a Harley-Davidson. This picture shows Richard doing several of his favourite things and was taken by Alan Benallick. The pair of them had gone to France to test ride and compare a Hyabusa with a Blackbird for an article, and they paused a while at this cafe for rest and refreshment.

Diesels have been experimented with for many years as power plants for motorcycles. Mr Freeman Sanders of Penzance made one from a 16H Norton in the early fifties, and used it regularly to go to Camborne College where he lectured. This is an Enfield with a Robin diesel engine that belongs to Peter Henshaw. Peter was for some years Editor of Motor Cycle Sport and Leisure, who under the ownership of Richard Stevens produced a wonderfully erudite magazine from offices based at Dennis Farm near St Columb.

Alan Bennallick and his all-Cornish appreciation Society in the Isle of Man. The bike is a bog standard 1000cc 2nd hand Yamaha R1 taken straight from the showroom of GT Motorcycles in Plymouth. The year was 1999 and in the Production TT Alan averaged 116.01 mph for 3 laps. From left to right the supporters are Richard, Ginger, Neal, Denzil, Stewart, Alan, Keith, Mike, Pam, Tadpole and Orville.

Above: Alan Benallick riding the RC30 750CC Honda in the Senior TT race in1998 where he finished 10th.

Opposite page: Opposite page: Alan Bennallick's first venture into road racing was when he was working for Camelford Bike Bits. Tony Powell helped sponsor this 750 Triumph, shown here at Thruxton in April 1990. Although Alan did try his hand at Hillclimbing (1985 Cornish 750 Champion), Grasstrack and briefly Motocross, road racing was his passion. He had a very successful career as a road racer, and went on to win the Manx Grand Prix Senior race on the Isle of Man in 1992.

Above: Part of a Cornish contigent visiting the Isle of Man in 1990. Amongst those present are Brian Colley, James Andrew, Paul Whetter, Barry Grose, Mark Seward and Johnathan Trevains.

Above: Left to right: Nick Palmer, John Deacon and Ian Graham in the 1994 Optic 2000, John Deacon's first ever desert race in Tunisia.

Above: Nick Palmer at the beginning of the 1994 event in St Tropez.

Left: John Deacon makes his debut in the Paris Dakar Race in 1998.

156

Nick Palmer of Callington flying the Cornish flag
in the desert, Tunisia.

John Deacon was not only a Cornish hero but had world recognition in the motorcycling world at 38 years of age. John, of Saltash, was killed in September 2001 whilst competing in the Master Rallye on his BMW R90RR. He was Britains most succesful competitor in the Dakar race, and was ten times British Enduro champion.

John Deacon - a Cornish Hero.

The GPS Satellite Navigation System essential for desert racing.

**Jim Jennings astride a Norton
built by Dennis Tresidder**